THE
MARY
BLACK
SONG BOOK

AS COMPILED BY
DECLAN SINNOTT

THE
AUTHORISED
VERSION

PUBLISHED BY DARA RECORDS
UNIT 4, GREAT SHIP STREET, DUBLIN 8, IRELAND
TEL: (01) 4781891. FAX: (01) 4782143

•

CONTENTS

•

I sometimes wonder what would have happened had I not met Declan Sinnott back in 1981. His knowledge and experience of music was invaluable to me then and remains so through six solo albums and twelve most enjoyable years of performing.

During those years the band of musicians, most of which are with me still, have played an important part in the development of the music and have become real friends to me.

Since the first solo album back in 1983 when we recorded Mick Hanly's "Crusader" we have made a conscious effort to record original songs by Irish songwriters. There has never been a shortage of good material to choose from and to the songwriters I am forever grateful.

This book contains a collection of some of the more popular songs from all of the albums. Finally thanks for your support over the years and I hope you enjoy singing these songs as much as I have.

When I first started to play I bought sheet music of my favourite songs often to find that they weren't accurate. It was very frustrating not to be sure you had the right chords.
In order to avoid this problem I have made sure these songs are in the right keys, have the same chords as the records and have piano arrangements that catch the atmosphere of the originals. I have also tried to keep it simple.
I'd like to thank Gerry McConnell for his painstaking work on the notation and also Frank Gallagher for the proof reading.
Mary and I are very happy with this book and hope you like it.

Declan Sinnott.

Anachie Gordon

(Trad. Arr. Mary Black) Little Rox Music

Medium Tempo

Hark - ing is bon - nie _____ and there lives__ my__ love _____

__ my__ heart lies on__ him__ and will__

__ not re - move _____ it will not__ re - move_

oh __ for __ all __ that I __ have done __ oh I

nev - er will __ for - get __ my love __ An - na - chie __

for An - na - chie __ Gor - don __ he's __

bon - nie and __ he's rough __ he'd en - tice a - ny

10

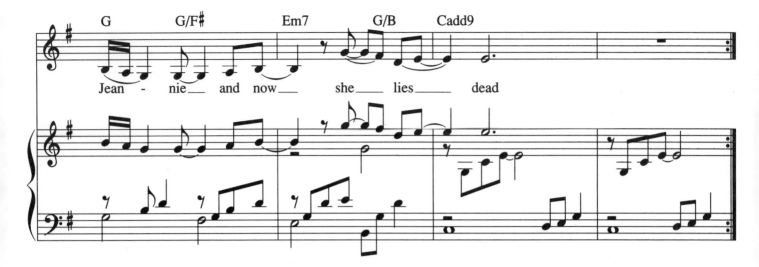

Jean - nie__ and now__ she__ lies__ dead

2. Down came her father and he's standing by the door
   Saying Jeannie you're trying the tricks of a whore
   You care nothing for a man who cares so very much for thee
   You must marry Lord Sulton and leave Anachie.
   For Anachie Gordon, he's barely but a man
   Although he may be pretty but where are his lands?
   Oh the Sultan's lands are broad and his towers they run high.
   You must marry Lord Sulton and leave Anachie.

3. With Anachie Gordon I'd beg for my bread,
   And before I'll marry Sulton it's gold to my head,
   With gold to my head and gowns fringed to the knee.
   And I'll die if I don't get me love Anachie.
   And you that are my parents to Church you may me bring
   But unto Lord Sulton I'll never bear a son.
   To a son or a daughter, I'll never bow my knee
   And I'll die if I don't get me love Anachie.

4. Jeannie was married and from church she was brought home
   And when she and her maidens so merry should have been
   When she and her maidens so merry should have been
   She went into her chamber she cries all alone.

5. Come to bed now Jeannie me honey and my sweet
   For to style you my mistress it would be so sweet
   Be it mistress or Jeannie it's all the same to me
   But in your bed Lord Sulton I never will lie.

6. The day Jeannie married was the day that Jeannie died
   And the day that young Anachie came home on the tide
   And down came her maidens all wringing of their hands
   Saying oh it's been so long you've spent so long on the sands.

7. You that are her maidens go take me by the hand
   And take me to the chamber that me love she lies in
   And he's kissed her cold lips till his heart has turned to stone
   And he's died in the chamber that his love she lies in.

Crusader

(Mick Hanly) Beann Eadair Music

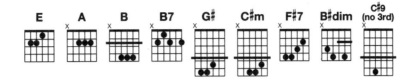

There's a wild - er - ness,__ it's a no-__man's land__ be - tween A - lice Springs__ and the o - cean

sev - en - teen__ hun - dred miles__ of burn - ing__ sand__ and a sil-

so

kiss the cheeks of your dear - est friends and turn to the des - ert a - head

now you're on your own like a sail -

- ing ship you're the cap - tain crew and the sail - ors

turn a round and this is what you see This is

me fac - ing me all a - lone 'cause I choose to be with the wind and the sun on me on - ly me now you dream

Now you dream so much about being lost
Your ghost by a coolebah sleeping
Haunts you and whispers in your ear
Give up give up this lonely road
No one knows the promise you're keeping
You can't touch the emptiness out here
But the grace that mends this broken wing
The blue sky to regain
Will lift those feet and raise those eyes
To face the desert again
As the dawn reveals the journey's end
In truth it's only beginning
And it's as big as your eyes wish to see
Chorus

Lovin' You

(J. Sebastian) Lieber/Stoller Songs/Carlin Music

17

run - nin' round fin - - gers on my fore - head could - n't calm me down_ and

I can't ev - en get me up and on my feet when

— I have to take care of some bus - 'ness on the

street _____ oh _____ I _ have _ been _ walk - in' _

all my streets a - lone___ I'd___ keep on___

walk - in'___ to keep from go - in'___ home___ I

could - n't quite bare - ly con - ceive of you now___ I can't con - ceive of ev - er

leav - in' you oh___ I'm___ just sit - tin' back sit - tin' here lov - in'___ you___

21

22

Song For Ireland

(Phil Colclough) Misty River Music

they know the call of free-dom in their breasts

saw Black Head a-gainst the

sky with twist-ed rocks that

run down to the sea liv-ing on your

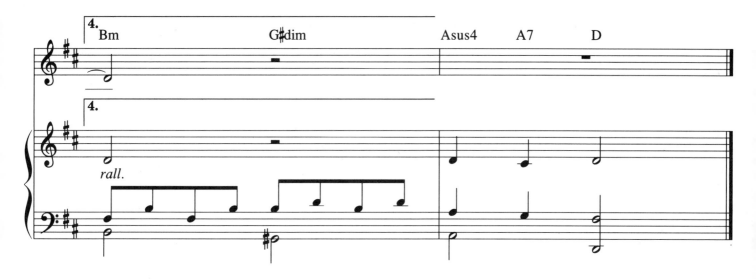

Talking all the day with true friends
Who try to make you stay
Telling jokes and news,
Singing songs to pass the night away
Stood on Dingle beach and cast
In wild foam we found Atlantic bass
Living on your western shore,
Saw summer sunsets, asked for more
I stood by your Atlantic sea
And sang a song for Ireland.

Drinking all the day in old pubs
Where fiddlers love to play
Someone touched the bow, he played a reel
It seemed so fine and gay
Watched the Galway salmon run
Like silver dancing darting in the sun
Living on your western shore,
Saw summer sunsets asked for more
I stood by your Atlantic sea
And sang a song for Ireland.

Dreaming in the night I saw a land
Where no man had to fight
Waking in your dawn
I saw you crying in the morning light
Lying where the falcons fly,
They twist and turn all in your e'er blue sky
Living on your western shore,
Saw summer sunsets asked for more
I stood by your Atlantic sea
And sang a song for Ireland.

Ellis Island

(Noel Brazil) Little Rox Music

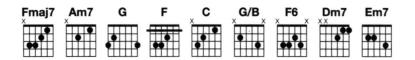

Moderately

From the

cor - ner of _ my eye _ I see a tear _ roll - ing down _ at the time _ I could - n't tell _ whose tear it was.

I'm ev-er gon-na hear you say____ good-bye____ babe__

good-bye_____ babe____

I hear____

cresc. . . . .

(mp)

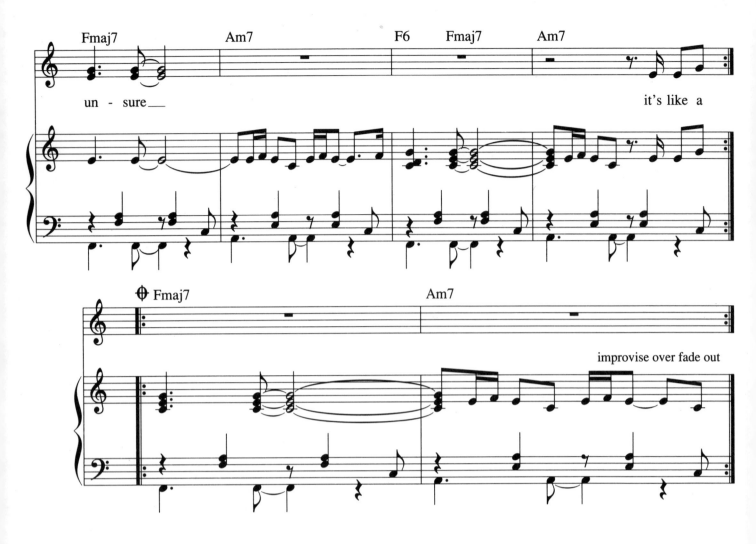

I hear sweethearts whisper their undying love
Above the noise on the quay their voices rise
They must have something so strong in the face of such change
That they can promise and promise all night
Oh their undying love, hear their undying love

This is the last call for Ellis Island
These are the last words I'm ever gonna hear you say
So goodbye babe, goodbye.

It's like a knife in my gut knowing you're taking leave
I feel I'm sentenced to a death without appeal
I can't pretend it's all a dream
And what I'm seeing will disappear
But the end I can see is all too real
Knowing you're taking leave
Knowing you're taking leave

This is the last call for Ellis Island
These are the last words I'm ever gonna hear you say
So goodbye babe, goodbye.
This is the last call for Ellis Island
These are the last words I'm ever gonna hear you say
So goodbye babe, goodbye.

Without the Fanfare

(Mick Hanly) Beann Eadair Music

33

2. By day I move words around like flowers
   I deliver by the afternoon
   'Cause the piper calls the tune
   Today I made full use of the hours
   I explored the smallest avenue
   And that feeling still came through
   Without the fanfare I love you.

4. Hello, do I still have you attention?
   I forgot to mention thanks again from the captain and the crew
   And so without the sweet perfume or roses
   I hope you can still believe it's true
   Stripped of all that much ado
   Without the fanfare I love you (2)

Once In A Very Blue Moon

(P. Alder/E. Levine) Bait & Bear Music/Michael Goldsen

(Tune guitar down a semitone to play with piano:
6th=D♯, 5th=G♯, 4th=C♯, 3rd=F♯, 2nd=A♯, 1st=D♯.)

2. No need to ask me if we can be friends
And help me right back on my feet again
And if I miss you well just now and then
Just once in a very blue moon
Just once in a very blue moon
Just once in a very blue moon
And I feel one coming on soon.

4. You act as if it doesn't hurt you at all
Like I'm the only one who's getting up from a fall
Don't you remember now don't you recall
Just once in a very blue moon
Just once in a very blue moon
Just once in a very blue moon
And I feel one coming on soon
Just once in a very blue moon.

By The Time It Gets Dark

(Sandy Denny) Jordiniere Music

41

We could go walkin' out in the sunshine
Look at all the people out in the street
Hurrying away to a business luncheon
Waiting for a taxi for aching feet
Light up your face baby let's get goin'
Want to see a change in those weary eyes
We'll have some fun take a boat out rowing
Why on earth should life be so serious?

Chorus

Katie

(Jimmy McCarthy) M.C.P.S.

Flowing, with feeling, not too slow

Tumb - ling curls_ of green_____ by stained glass stream - ing light_

— and a yel - low col - oured lamp - shade used_ to

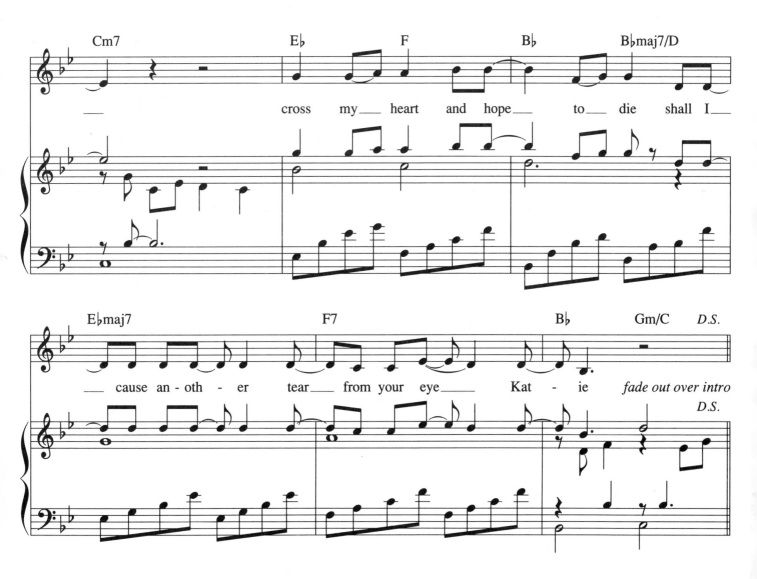

The mirror that won't talk and your nightgown on the door
And the old pedal singer just don't sing no more
You can roll the reels for hours
From the movie of this book
It's a question mark on this heart of mine
Sends an elder back to look

Come running home again, Katie
Come running home again
Cross my heart and hope to die
Shall I cause another tear from your eye Katie

Now I'm looking through a tunnel
Back into the room
With the genius of a druid when the sunlight floods the tomb
And I'm never going back there, and I couldn't anyway
'Cause though I made the great escape
I never got away

Come running home Katie
Come running home again
Cross my heart and hope to die
Shall I cause another tear from your eye

Come running home again, Katie
Come running home again
Cross my heart and hope to die
Shall I cause another tear from your eye Katie

Carolina Rua (The Crooked Road)

(Thom Moore) Little Rox Music

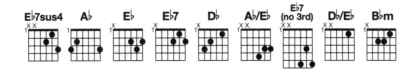

Lively feel

Stor - ies nev - er end 'til you come___ to con - clus-

___ions: oh Car - o - lin - a ruadh___ has a hand___

Oh standing on three queens, thought the game was over
Then, in from the blue, Carolina's at my shoulder
Oh laughter in her eyes and a smile that touches all the guys

Oh down the windy road where my Carolina goes
Oh down the crooked road where Carolina goes to school
Mo Carolina Rua, tell me...

Oh Carolina Rua has my heart and all I want to do is
Go down the windy road where my Carolina goes
Down the crooked road where Carolina goes to school
Mo Carolina Rua, do you love me?
Tell me true. Tell me...

Columbus

(Noel Brazil) Little Rox Music

lum - bus

with an ache___ in your tra - vel - ling heart___

tide___ must ebb and flow I am dragged_____ down

under and I wait_____ the live - long____ day for an end____

_____ to my____ hun - ger_____ so I dream____ of Co -

2. See how the cormorant swoops and dives
Must be some thrill to go that deep
Down to the basement of this life
Down to where the mermaid gently sleeps
Not like here in this blue light
Far away from the fireside
Where things can get twisted and haunted and crowded
You can't even feel alright

Chorus
So you dream of Columbus
Every time that the panic starts
You dream of Columbus
With your maps and your beautiful charts
You dream of Columbus
With an ache in your travelling heart

3. And as the tide must ebb and flow
I am dragged down under
And I wait the livelong day
For an end to my hunger

Chorus

No Frontiers

(Jimmy McCarthy) M.C.P.S.

If your life is a rough bed of brambles and nails
And your spirit's a slave to man's whips and man's jails
Where you thirst and you hunger for justice and right
Then your heart is a pure flame of man's constant night
In your eyes faint as the singing of a lark
That somehow this black night
Feels warmer for the spark
Warmer for the spark
To hold us 'til the day when fear will lose its grip
And heaven has its way

Heaven knows no frontiers
And I've seen heaven in your eyes
Heaven knows no frontiers
And I've seen heaven in your eyes.

Past The Point Of Rescue

(Mick Hanly) Beann Eadair Music

68

2. Days like a slow train trickle by
Even the words that I write refuse to fly
All that I can hear is your song haunting me
Can't get the melody out of my head you see
Distractions I've been using
Do you know how much you're losing
No you don't, but I do

Bright Blue Rose

(Jimmy McCarthy) M.C.P.S.

she like a ghost be-side me goes down with the ease of a dol-phin

and e-merg-es un-learned un-shamed un-harmed for

she is the per-fect crea-ture nat-ur-al in ev-'ry fea-ture and

I am the geek with the al-chem-ist's stone

for all of you___ who must___ dis - cov - er___

for all who seek to un - der - stand___

for___ hav - ing left the path___ of___ oth - ers___ you'll

___ find___ a ver - y spec - ial___ hand___ and

73

it is__ a ho - ly thing__ and__ it is__ a prec - ious time__ and

it is the on - ly__ way for -

get - me - nots_ a - mong_ the snow_ it's al - ways been__ and so it goes_ to

pon - der__ his death and__ his__ life e - ter - nal - ly__

For all of you who must discover
For all who seek to understand
For having left the path of others
You'll find a very special hand

And it is a holy thing, and it is a precious time
And it is the only way
Forget-me-nots among the snow, it's always been and so it goes
To ponder his death and his life eternally

One bright blue rose outlives all those
Two thousand years and still it goes
To ponder his death and his life eternally

Babes In The Wood

(Noel Brazil) Little Rox Music

Bright tempo, not too fast

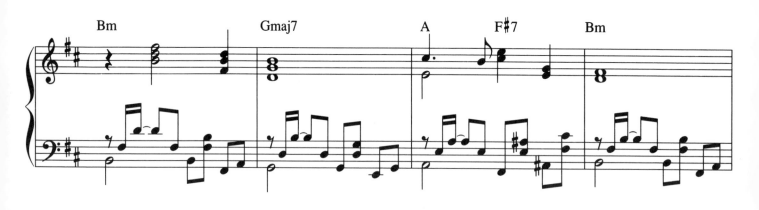

Babes in the wood walk-in' thru snow

big__ bad wolf at the win - dow

not much choice__ in the mat - ter now__

__ some must lead__ some must fol -

__ low

a touch can mean dis - tance to__ some peo -

- ple

a touch__ can mean pri - son or be like a cage__

that's an-oth-er stor-y   this is their stor-y

this is their stor-y

this is___ this is___ this is_____ their stor - y

Babes in the wood. Eager and keen
Soft as the fern underneath them
Wet to the skin from their own hot glow
No more wolf at the window

Touch can mean distance to some people
Touch can mean I own you forever and a day
If only life could be more simple
Especially in this day and age

They got the time, They got the need
The world's getting weird, The wolf's running free
But that's another story, This is their story

But touch can be a blessing to other people
Touch can bring blossom to things that decay
I think life should be that simple
Especially in this day and age

They got the time, They got the need
The world's getting weird. The wolf's running free
But that's another story. This is, This is their story

Adam At The Window

(Jimmy McCarthy) M.C.P.S.

of sun-light slow-ly trick-le down___ the curve of lips her fin - ger tips___ in kiss - ing sips we___ drown in kiss-ing sips we drown___ and A - dam will have his way___ A - dam will have his

way _____ will have his way A - dam

Adam's on the island
Living in the land of love
Shadows lurk around him
Drunk of the royal jelly of pure love
Full and ripe the fruit hang
For when the prince arrives he will want more
And more and more he'll drink from the canvas cup
The son of a swan will then lose his plumera
And he will wear a new age suit
And haunt the joints in town
And play a silver magic flute
And call his lovers down
And call his lovers down

And Adam will have his way
Adam will have his way
Adam will have his way

Adam's at the easel
Painting in the wrinkles and the grey
Waiting for November
Easy with the darkness of the day
Smiles a tear of gladness
And Adam's at the window once again
Burning in the sunlight

Too late to wait
For darkness won't delay
To steal her cherry lips away
For while the careless tongues of sunlight
Slowly trickle down
The curve of hips, her fingertips
In kissing sips we drown
In kissing sips we drown

Chorus:
And Adam will have his way
Adam will have his way
Adam will have his way

Thorn Upon The Rose

(Julie Mathews) Circuit Music Ltd.

and you're still reel-ing from the feel-ing when he's gone___

the door is closed___ the lock is turned___ and all___ the mem-o-ries___ and

let-ters have been burned   so   when   you___pick the___ hand-some flow-er

don't for - get____ the thorn up - on____ the rose____ it's cut is deep and____ it's scar____

____ lasts for ev - er   it fol - lows love____ where   ev - er love goes____

just how we fall   ev - er love____

goes

win or lose _____ it"s just the

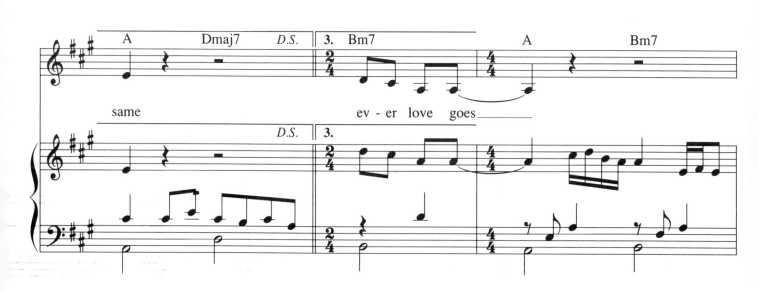

same   ev - er love goes _____

Just how we fall it's hard to know
When what we feel we seldom show
So we show the parts we feel are best
We squirm around the edges trying to cover up the rest
And you think you know him and he thinks the same
When underneath it all it's just a crazy guessing game

Chorus

Win or lose it's just the same
Tears of joy tears of pain
They're hand in hand they come as one
You'll never see the moon without the promise of the sun
For all the bruises for all the blows
I'd rather feel the thorn than to never see the rose

Chorus...

Only A Woman's Heart

(Eleanor McEvoy) Little Rox Music/Dandelion Music

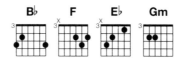

as on - ly a wom-

an   as on - ly___ a wom - an   as

on - ly___ a wom - an's___ heart___ can___ be___

3. Dal 𝄋

B♭ **Verse**

the tears___ that drip   from

Verse

my ___ own _____ my

When restless eyes
Reveal my troubled soul
And memories flood my weary heart
I mourn for my dreams
I mourn for my wasted love
And while I know that I'll survive alone

Chorus
My heart is low, My heart is so low
As only a woman's heart can be
As only a woman's, As only a woman's
As only a woman's heart can know

My heart is low, My heart is so low
As only a woman's heart can be
As only a woman's, as only a woman's
As only a woman's heart can know